THE HUNS HAVE GOT MY GRAMOPHONE!

THE HUNS

HAVE GOT MY

GRAMOPHONE!

ADVERTISEMENTS FROM THE GREAT WAR

Amanda-Jane Doran
and Andrew McCarthy

Bodleian Library
UNIVERSITY OF OXFORD

ISBN 978 1 85124 399 0

Cover and text design by Dot Little
Typeset in 10½ on 12½ Adobe Garamond by illuminati, Grosmont
Printed and bound by C&C offset Printing Company Ltd., Hong Kong,
on 100 gsm Chinese Sen Po Enlanda 1.7 paper

British Library Catalogue in Publishing Data
A CIP record of this publication is available from the British Library

Contents

Punch, 7 June 1911, p. xix

Introduction

⟨⟩

GREAT BRITAIN in 1914 was a rich and powerful
country, the centre of an empire that covered
one quarter of the world's land surface. The Industrial Revolution had created the skills and machinery
which could make a wide range of products, from
motor cars to gramophones, from fountain pens
to processed food. Some well-known twenty-first-
century brands – such as Rolls-Royce, Burberry
and Perrier – were well established, but these firms
had spent heavily on advertising, and any firm that
wanted to prosper needed to make its name and
products as widely known as possible. In 1914 this
meant posters, and advertisements in newspapers
and magazines. There was no radio broadcasting, no
television. There were thirteen national daily papers,
and several weekly illustrated news magazines such
as the *Graphic* and the *Illustrated London News*.
The rapid national distribution of daily papers had
become possible from 1838 onwards as the railway
network developed, and railways could distribute
nationally advertised goods quickly and cheaply.
The pages of *Punch* and the *Illustrated London
News* were packed with advertisements for patent
medicines to help you feel better, ladies' frocks and
gentlemen's raincoats to make you look better, and

THIS IS NOT AN A.S.C. MAN GUARDING STORES. IT IS MERELY AN AVERAGE INFANTRYMAN WITH THE ORDINARY ALLOWANCE OF COMMODITIES, IF WE ARE TO BELIEVE THE ADVERTISERS' ACCOUNT OF WHAT IS INDISPENSABLE.

Punch, 15 December 1915, p. 481

whisky and cigarettes to help you to relax. Advertising for breakfast cereals was so frenzied that Hector Hugh Munro, 'Saki', wrote a story about Pipenta, an inedible breakfast cereal that was about to bankrupt its manufacturer because he had spent so much on advertising. A struggling artist wants to marry the manufacturer's daughter, and is told that he may, if he is able to sell 'that beastly muck'. The artist renames the product Filboid Studge, and produces a poster of the Damned in Hell, with the slogan 'They cannot buy it now'. Filboid Studge flies off the shelves, and the manufacturer withdraws his consent to the marriage as his daughter is now a wealthy heiress.

Punch, 23 December 1914, p. vii

The last time that Prussia had invaded France, in 1870, advertisements in the *Illustrated London News* were columns of small print 2½ inches (6.5 cm) wide, with no illustrations. When advertisers began to use illustrations in the 1880s, they would introduce a small drawing of their product, surrounded by dense type. As literacy increased during the nineteenth century, Britain had led the world in the production of illustrated books and magazines. Advertisers began to use larger illustrations of a similar quality to those that had been drawn to accompany the works of Dickens and Thackeray. S.H. Benson, who set up his advertising agency in 1893, with Bovril as his first client, had pioneered the more stylish

approach. In 1896 the *Illustrated London News*
satirized the 'New Craze for Artistic Posters', with a
cartoon showing people in evening dress admiring a
Bovril poster at a private view. Benson believed that
a campaign should have a definite objective, rather
than just reminding people that a product existed.

In 1914 some advertisements still looked like
those of the 1880s, but the best, such as those for
Boots the Chemists, seized the reader's attention
with a picture that distinguished the product from
its rivals. Commercial artists often drew for both
magazine publishers and advertisers, which provided
a continuity of style. Advertisers had to make their
goods stand out in a crowded market, as the cartoon
of the soldier with his pile of stores reminds us.

In November 1914 Winston Churchill said
that the motto of the British people was 'Business
carried on as usual during alterations on the map of
Europe', and so it proved. Advertisers were quick to
respond to the war. Thresher & Glenny advertised
'Active Service Kits' in *The Times* on 4 August 1914,
and in *Punch* on 16 September De Reszke showed
a young woman bidding farewell to a naval officer
with a gift of cigarettes. These were existing brands,
which were now being advertised with the war
in mind, but it was not long before entirely new
products appeared. Thresher & Glenny created the
'Trench Coat', 'designed for present conditions of
warfare', and placed the first advertisement for it in
Punch on 23 December 1914. This was quick work.
The British Expeditionary Force had only begun to

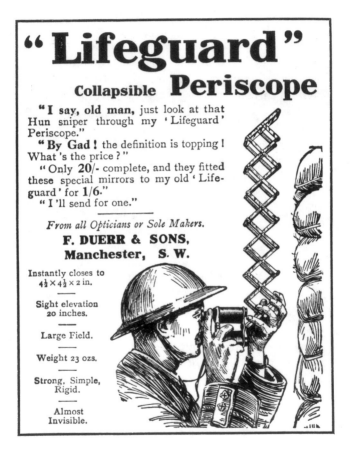

"Lifeguard"
Collapsible Periscope

"**I say, old man,** just look at that Hun sniper through my 'Lifeguard' Periscope."

"**By Gad!** the definition is topping! What's the price?"

"Only **20/-** complete, and they fitted these special mirrors to my old 'Lifeguard' for **1/6**."

"I'll send for one."

From all Opticians or Sole Makers.

F. DUERR & SONS,
Manchester,   S. W.

Instantly closes to
$4\frac{1}{2} \times 4\frac{1}{2} \times 2$ in.

Sight elevation
20 inches.

Large Field.

Weight 23 ozs.

Strong, Simple,
Rigid.

Almost
Invisible.

Punch, 23 August 1916, p. iii

entrench on the Aisne fourteen weeks earlier. The
advertisement on page 9 stresses the coat's advantages, but the layout is poorly designed. Thresher's
placed similar advertisements in early 1915, but they
knew they had to make their trench coats stand
out. At least fourteen firms advertised officers'
waterproofs, and some began making trench coats as
well. In early 1915 Burberry and Aquascutum had the
most stylish advertisements. By November Thresher's
had developed the style they used for the rest of
the war, showing a dashing officer like the ones on
pages 20, 83 and 84. On 9 July 1916 *Punch* printed a
cartoon by Fougasse, 'War's Brutalising Influence',
comparing a pre-war 'fashion plate' advertisement
for officers' kit with a rugged officer very like the
advertisement on page 20. The new style continued
after the war. In 1925 a Thresher advertisement
showed the officer on page 20 in pale tones, with the
same man in civilian clothes, in black and white, in
front of him. The slogan, 'We Made Your Thresher
Trenchcoat', is saying 'You trusted us on the Somme,
trust us again in peacetime.'

In 1913 the War Office had hired Hedley Le Bas
to increase army recruitment. Le Bas, the founder
of Caxton Publishing, had introduced modern
advertising methods to bookselling. When war
broke out, he said that the army had been advertising for soldiers for at least a hundred years, but the
old methods – such as suggesting that strong drink
was cheaper abroad – would certainly not appeal
to Lord Kitchener, the Secretary of State for War.

Kitchener had a very moral view of what a soldier ought to be. Le Bas knew that Kitchener's name and reputation would bring in recruits. Kitchener had won wars, and looked like a soldier. Le Bas said: 'The people trusted him. ... The right to use the name made the enormous task of finding a new army all the easier.'

The lieutenant who is looking at 'Hun snipers' through his periscope, and the officer who complains that the Huns have got his gramophone, used the word 'Hun' because of a speech given by Kaiser Wilhelm II at Bremerhaven on 27 July 1900. Wilhelm, Queen Victoria's grandson, was regarded favourably enough in Britain in 1911 for his picture to be used in the De Reszke advertisement. Despite this, he was well known for making offensive speeches. His courtiers made frantic efforts to keep his words out of the newspapers, but they always failed. At Bremerhaven he had addressed German marines who were about to embark for China as part of an international force to suppress the Boxer Rebellion. 'No pardon will be given! Prisoners will not be taken!' 'Just as the Huns under their King Etzel [Attila] acquired a reputation a thousand years ago which makes them appear mighty even today in tradition and fairy tales, so, through you may the name of the Germans resonate in China a thousand years hence, so that no Chinaman will ever again dare look askance at a German!' After this, in the British popular press the Germans were 'Huns', capable of any atrocity, real or imagined.

Advertisers were selling to soldiers in the front line and to soldiers' relations. Some advertisements play on the guilt of those at home, using exhortations such as 'Save the Lives of Our Men by Sending Them the Anti-Live Barbed Wire Glove', or by asking 'Is that Tyre Made in Your Own Country?' Frequent use was made of 'Send a Tin to Your Soldier Friend', which could be adapted to many products. All three fountain-pen advertisements in this book are aimed at friends and relations, as are two of the gramophone advertisements. Many officers used fountain pens and gramophones in the trenches, unlike some gadgets of doubtful effectiveness such as the body shield. Periscopes really were used and requested by front-line soldiers, and it is interesting that the copy in the advertisement on page 11 is written as if one soldier is speaking to another. The memoirs of Siegfried Sassoon, Charles Carrington and Robert Graves give fascinating accounts of which equipment fighting soldiers really needed. Gadgets such as ear defenders and body armour were discarded in favour of wire-cutters, electric torches and pistols.

Before the war few women had an independent income. As women began to take the jobs of men who had joined up, advertisers realized that some of them, especially munition workers, had money to spend on themselves. Willys Overland advertised cars in 1915 with the slogan 'Your wife can drive it', but by 1918 Douglas were advertising motorcycles directly to female munition workers, knowing that the women could afford them. Women's fashion advertisements changed, reflecting the fact that women had jobs that had previously been done by men.

By 1918 the cost of food and clothing had doubled. Income tax had increased by 260 per cent, to 6 shillings (30p) in the pound. Advertising had become more professional, and more stylish. Some advertisements were still messy and ill designed, but the firms that wanted to prosper knew that they had to use the best agencies, copywriters and artists that they could to survive in the post-war world. The developments during the Great War, as the examples in this book illustrate, had changed the face of advertising for good.

Land and Water, 28 August 1915, p. 387

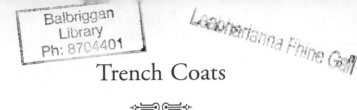

Trench Coats

I T IS hard to imagine a world unadorned by
the trench coat: familiar to us as a twenty-first-
century fashion staple or as an indispensable form of
protection from the weather for officers during the
Great War. Before 1914 the trench coat, as we would
recognize it, did not exist. It emerged as a hybrid,
customized from Boer War field coats, army great-
coats and Burberry sports apparel. Its origins are
fascinating. The trench coat is a direct descendant of
the nineteenth-century radical dress-reform movement, which promoted comfortable, unrestricted
clothing, ease of movement, natural fabrics and
'rational and artistic' styling.

The development of practical, weatherproof
clothing was pioneered by Thomas Burberry, whose
windproof and rainproof textiles and garments were
designed for farmers and sportsmen. In 1879 Burberry invented gabardine, a twill fabric waterproofed
before weaving and tailoring. The polar explorers
Amundsen, Shackleton and Captain Scott all put
Burberry's fabrics and clothing to the extreme test.
Lords Kitchener and Baden-Powell wore voluminous
and single-breasted Burberry weatherproofs during
the South African wars. Durable, warm and lightweight, these were made from the first high-tech

sports fabrics. Early in the twentieth century they were already being adapted for use on the battlefield, an application Burberry may have had misgivings about, given his passionately held Baptist beliefs. From 1917 until his death in 1926 he devoted himself to religious and humanitarian activities.

The weather conditions at the front dictated the type of battle dress and weaponry used. The winter of 1914 was atrocious, with gales and floods. This had followed on from a hot and sultry summer and autumn, when armies had been on the move. By 16 September Sir John French had given orders to entrench on the River Aisne. In early December 1914 an officer writing in *The Times* published his 'Hints to Officers Called to the Front'. Trench life had begun, and advice about dress and equipment was vital for those about to leave for active service: 'a sword is a very uncommon object in the field. It is inconvenient to carry; it is very awkward to tuck away in a trench, and when one is at close quarters with the enemy it is distinctly inferior to a bayonet. I would personally rather carry a battleaxe.' He continues: 'it is best to carry a greatcoat or a Burberry … I prefer the latter – the going is very bad.'

Waterproofs were never regulation army issue, and only officers were allowed to wear them over their army uniforms. They were popular items, in spite of their expense. A waterproof coat cost between £2 10 shillings (£2.50) for a Dunhill short trench mac and 4 guineas (£4.20) for an unlined Burberry. A Thresher lined with sheepskin was 8

BURBERRY TRENCH OUTFIT

ARMOUR OF PROOF
A complete safeguard for Officers against the terrible hardships of the trenches.

OFFICERS AT THE FRONT
have supplied data for the design throughout—men experienced in what is essential during excessive exposure in trench warfare.

BURBERRY TRENCH KIT
is absolutely impervious to rain, sleet, snow, or water,

*YET PERFECTLY SELF-VENTILATING.
Biting winds cannot penetrate its densely-woven fabric, and for this reason

SIR E. SHACKLETON,
Capt. Scott, Capt. Amundsen and Sir Douglas Mawson used it on their expeditions to the South Pole as the chief protection against the fierce cold and extraordinary gales of those dreaded regions.

*NOTE.—Oiled interlinings are as impervious to air as Rabbits. They are not used by Burberrys because they are dangerous to health and not necessary in a Burberry coat.

BURBERRY TRENCH KIT
consists of a
BURBERRY TRENCH-WARM—combines the services of THREE coats in ONE, each of which can be worn separately. **A WEATHERPROOF that keeps out any rain that an oilskin keeps out ;** a Camel Fleece SHORT-WARM ; and a thick, double-fronted OVERCOAT for the severest weather.
CAP COVER AND CAPE—a covering for head and neck: an extra protection over the shoulders, preventing any possibility of wet entering at the collar.
GABARDINE SHORTS worn as illustrated, under The Trench-Warm prevent wet dripping on the breeches.
GABARDINE GLOVES, lined Wool, worn with the gauntlet inside the sleeves of the coat, and
BURBERRY TRENCH BOOTS complete this staunch and dependable outfit for the Officer in the trenches.

Everything the Officer needs ready for immediate use

or completed to measure in from 2 to 4 days.

Uniforms from £5 5s. in Serge; £6 6s. in Whipcord.
Special quotations made to Regiments.

Illustrated Military or Naval Catalogues Post Free

BURBERRYS Haymarket LONDON
also 8 and 10 Boulevard Malesherbes PARIS.

Land and Water, 10 February 1916, p. 23

THE THRESHER

For Comfort, Security and Service at any period of the year rely on a Thresher and make sure it bears the label Thresher & Glenny

The original Trench Coat designed by Charles Glenny in October, 1914, was brought to the notice of all Officers commanding Corps by the War Office the first winter of the War. It fills the functions of a Great Coat, British Warm, and Raincoat, and the measure of its success may be gauged by the quantity of imitations. Over 8,200 genuine Threshers worn by British Officers.

Trench Coat with detachable " Kamelcott " lining.

£5 10 0

Trench Coat, unlined,

£4 14 6

Mounted pattern, 15/6 extra

Send size of chest and approximate height when ordering. All sizes in stock

THRESHER & GLENNY
152 & 153, Strand, LONDON, W.C.
Military Tailors and Outfitters.

Bystander, 2 August 1916, p. 217

guineas (£8.40). There was a great deal of competition between rival outfitters and tailors to provide waterproof topcoats to protect officers from the elements. Burberry's Burfron and Tielocken vied with Aquascutum's waterproof field coat, which was tailored in wool; the featherlight 'Hurricane Smock' cost 67 shillings and sixpence (£3.37½), and was manufactured in Liverpool.

The first coat to be called a 'Trench Coat' was made by Thresher & Glenny, 'Military Tailors and Outfitters' founded in 1683, based in the Strand in Central London. They advertised service kit in *Punch* regularly and on 23 December 1914 a new garment with a new name was advertised in the magazine for the first time. The Thresher 'Trench Coat' was born, and described, importantly, as 'Wind, Wet & Mud resisting', 6 guineas (£6.30) with Kamelkott lining. It was made of hard khaki drill, was double breasted and had a stand-up, storm-proof collar. This became the preferred pattern, as exemplified in the fashion and tailoring journal the *West End Gazette* for October 1915. Halfway through the conflict in September 1916 Thresher & Glenny were proudly advertising that ten thousand of their eponymous coats had been sold.

As the war progressed and conditions at the front worsened, the trench coat was adapted in various ways, and was significantly shortened. Once women were encouraged into war service by the Board of Trade in March 1915 they also needed uniforms and protective clothing. The trench coat provided the

perfect outerwear and the *Tatler* used editorial and advertising space to extol its virtues. By 1917 there were different designs from Jaeger, Turnbull & Asser and many others. Samuel Brothers Universal Outfitters ran a charming advertisement entitled 'A Trench-Ant Reflection', showing an officer of a Highland regiment in tartan gaiters and tam-o'-shanter admiring his trench coat in a full-length mirror; the image gazing back in the mirror is of a young woman dressed almost identically, whose choice of coat is described as 'eminently sane, stylish and sensible'. Could this be the first real example of unisex clothing? This is a ground-breaking image and indicative of the leap that women of the period were making towards equality, with similar oc-cupations to men and the same needs and clothing requirements. This is reflected in Barker's advertise-ment for women's service kit.

For the last two years of the war the 'Trencher' was adopted by both sexes as utilitarian rainwear and, simultaneously, as a popular, high-fashion garment. It was no longer a luxury item, but pur-chasable in a variety of styles and fabrics for every budget. Ironically, it was not available to the ordi-nary soldier, who had most need of it at the front.

Scotsman, 9 July 1915

Food and Drink

❖⇒◎⇐❖

M ANY OF the foods consumed at home and
on the front between 1914 and 1918 are still
household names today. Oxo cubes, Lea & Perrins'
sauce, Crawford's biscuits and Wincarnis tonic wine
were nourishing, familiar and soothing. Troops and
civilians needed fortifying; the emotional role of
sustenance from drinks such as Bovril and Ovaltine
was as important as the physical one. Later on, as
food shortages took hold, manufacturers also played a
big part in encouraging food economy.

The young men who presented themselves for
military training with the Royal Warwickshires to be
'converted into soldiers' in 1918 had not all had the
benefits of good food. 'The sallow, shambling, fright-
ened victims of our industrial system' were transformed
after six months of hearty meals, drilling and field
exercises. They put on weight and even grew taller
under the military regime. In his memoir, *Soldier from
the Wars Returning*, Charles Carrington averred 'it is
enough to make me into a violent socialist … when I
see what soldiering makes of them.'

Every effort was made to keep men well fed on
active service. The diet could, however, become mono-
tonous, especially in the front line, where supplies of
fresh, hot food could not be relied upon. Hot tea, cold

Appetizing meals in the Trenches

Your soldier friends will appreciate the gift of a few bottles of Lea & Perrins' Sauce to use with their War Rations. It makes Bully Beef appetizing, and when mixed with jam is an excellent substitute for chutnee. Messrs. Lea & Perrins will send *One Dozen Special Bottles* (half ordinary size)

Lea & Perrins' Sauce

(the original and genuine Worcestershire) securely packed direct to any member of the Expeditionary Force on the Western Front, Carriage Paid, for 5s.

The case will be forwarded immediately on receipt of postal order with full name and regimental address of intended recipient.

LEA & PERRINS, 32, Midland Rd., WORCESTER.

Carriage **Paid** *direct to the Western Front for* **5/-**

Daily Express, 23 December 1915, p. 2

Tatler, 12 September 1917, p. i

stew, hard biscuits softened with Tickler's plum and apple jam were the order of the day. Worcestershire sauce enlivened the ubiquitous Maconochie's tinned stew of indeterminate meat, potatoes, beans and vegetables. Bovril was an appetizing luxury; Wincarnis was, surprisingly, fortified with Liebig (German) meat extract. The supply chain behind the lines was a marvel of organization. Canteens produced meals on an industrial scale. Each day 60 tons of food arrived in parcels from relatives of the fighting men.

At home and in France rabbits and wild game were fair game, other meat was scarce. Oxo published recipes which were cheap, filling and gave a savoury illusion. 'Potato Pears' could be prepared from mashed potato, breadcrumbs, parsley and salt, and shaped and garnished with a clove. Instructions for serving: 'garnished with or without rolls of fried bacon' (mostly without, one assumes).

Luxuries were available from exclusive suppliers, including Fortnum & Mason and Twining's. Formosa Oolong tea was aimed at the wealthy who still expected silver service and dainty cakes for afternoon tea. Cafés and restaurants were serving working people of all classes who had money to spend, and food had to be found. The all-male bastions of gentlemen's clubs had fallen; young women provided essential staffing. Tea dances also brought new freedom to many young people, who were mixing beyond their own narrow social confines for the first time. Society was on the verge of enormous change, to be brought about by the exigencies of war.

Tatler, 6 June 1917, p. 321

Women and Motor Vehicles

IN JULY 1897 two female journalists from the *Gentlewoman* set out from Arthur Mulliner's coachworks in Northampton to drive a Daimler to London. This was one of the first press trials of any car, and 'the longest car journey yet undertaken by women'. At first Mulliner drove. When asked why he called the car 'she', he said that it took a man to manage her. 'Nonsense!' said the women, and they both took turns at driving, steering with the tiller, a right-angled bar that protruded from the bonnet. Steering wheels would not be introduced until 1898. The 80-mile journey took 8½ hours, including a stop for lunch (*Gentlewoman*, 17 July and 24 July 1897).

Motoring could be hazardous. If the front wheels hit a pothole, the tiller would be jerked out of the driver's hands. Engines had to be started by hand-cranking. This required considerable physical strength and skill. When you crank-start an engine, you must not grasp the starting-handle as you would do naturally. The thumb must lie in the same direction as the fingers. If the engine does not ignite properly, it can run backwards for a short way. If your thumb is on the wrong side of the handle, it will get broken. With wonderful British understatement, the Brolt advertisement describes

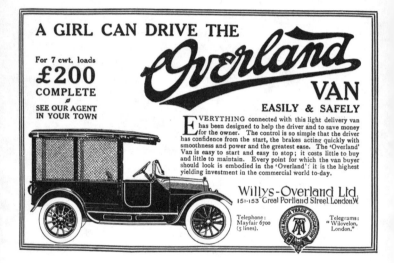

Punch, 6 December 1916, p. vii

this procedure as 'tiresome'. Electric self-starters were advertised in the USA in 1911 with the slogan 'Any woman can start your car', implying that women did not own cars. Six years later the Brolt advertisement refers to 'your car', and shows a woman driver cranking the car.

Willys-Overland was an American company, and was in the enviable position of having cars to sell, because it was not making vehicles for the British Army. The USA did not declare war on Germany until April 1917. Willys-Overland understood how to market their vehicles in a way that many British manufacturers did not. 'A Girl Can Drive the Overland Van' appealed to business-owners whose drivers had joined up, although the assumption seems to be that women, and girls, do not buy vans. The advertisement stresses the ease with which the van can be driven. It is not really a van, but a car with a van body. Willys-Overland had used the same technique to sell their £225 car in 1915: 'Your wife can drive it.' The copy stresses ease of driving, and that the car comes with an electric starter and all accessories.

Douglas advertised their motorcycles to female munition workers – there are shells in the background of the picture to this advertisement – knowing that they had enough money to buy one themselves. Munition workers were paid up to £5 a week on Tyneside in 1916.

The need of the armed services for drivers provided opportunities for women which could not have been imagined in 1897. The Women's

Do YOU ride a

Douglas

Hundreds of lady war workers are using the handy little Douglas Motor Cycle almost every day for business purposes. The Douglas saves them time and travelling expenses.

Why not write to-day for a copy of our Catalogue to Dept. "M."

DOUGLAS MOTORS, LTD., KINGSWOOD, BRISTOL.

Graphic, 20 July 1918, p. 34

Volunteer Reserve had been set up in 1914, and sought to enrol 'qualified motorists, motor-cyclists, and aviators' aged 16–40. Classified advertisements appeared for 'chauffeuse–companions' who could drive, do running repairs and act as companions to their lady employers. Any woman who could afford the £21 charged by the Hon. Gabrielle Borthwick for a comprehensive motor-maintenance and driving course at her workshops near Piccadilly could learn how to dismantle an engine, grind valves, cut screws, solder and braze. That went well beyond running repairs.

A woman with those skills would hardly be satisfied with work as a chauffeuse–companion at 25 shillings (£1.25) a week. Muriel Thompson had won the first motor race for women at Brooklands in 1908, averaging 50 m.p.h. In January 1915 she joined the FANY (First Aid Nursing Yeomanry) as an ambulance driver. The British Army would not accept women drivers on the front line, so she worked for the French and the Belgians. The British relented in January 1916. In January 1918 Muriel Thompson was made commander of a joint FANY and VAD (Voluntary Aid Detachment) ambulance unit at St Omer. In May 1918 the Germans bombed Arques heavily. An ammunition dump was hit, and shells began to explode. The women were ordered to take cover, but they carried on evacuating the wounded. Sixteen Military Medals and three Croix de Guerre were awarded to the female ambulance drivers for their bravery. Muriel Thompson was awarded both medals.

Medicines

❖⟾◉⟾❖

I F THERE is one medical condition that has characterized the First World War for posterity it is neurasthenia. Seldom used today, it is an anachronistic term that encompassed a wide range of nervous complaints, superficial and profound, including shell shock.

Its origins lie at the end of the nineteenth century, when the disease was identified by American neurologist George Beard. Beard maintained that the increasing number of cases of nervous breakdown were caused by the speed and fragmentation of modern industrialized life. He specified six causes: 'steam power, the periodical press, the telegraph, the sciences, the mental activity of women and the erosion of religious faith'. Causes and cures were equally ambiguous. Nourishing food, rest and, in the example of neurasthenia, electrical current were offered to ameliorate the condition.

After four punishing years of conflict, the symptoms detailed in the advertisement for the Pulvermacher Electrological Institute's appliances must have been very common across the British Isles. There is no indication whether the treatment is aimed at servicemen as well as the general public. The mental strain of mechanized warfare

on an unprecedented scale was injuring civilians
and soldiers in new ways. Shell shock was initially
defined by the supposed physical impact of nearby
artillery on the brain; the concept of independent
psychological damage did not really exist at the
beginning of the war. Its treatment was haphazard
and experimental. The situation gradually improved
and by the end of 1916 psychiatric treatment was
available on 'mental wards' in army hospitals. After
the war was over it was another matter; there was no
national health service to support the physically and
mentally broken.

Many and various were the patent medicines
and herbal preparations available 'over the counter'
between 1914 and 1918. They had no guarantee of
any efficacy in modern scientific terms. In the nineteenth century fortunes were made on the vast sales
of such pills, which were usually laxatives. Herbert
Ingram, who launched the *Illustrated London News*
in 1842, funded the magazine on the proceeds of his
Parr's Life Pills, which could 'conquer disease and
prolong life'.

Jubol was marketed in a similar way, although
there were fewer coy euphemisms in twentieth-
century magazine advertisements. Victorian advertising never mentioned specific bowel problems or
referred to parts of the body, interior or exterior. As
the war progressed, medical matters and treatments
became common topics for discussion. Scientific
advances were invoked as a selling point. The
emphasis here is on the 're-education of the intestine'

and vague medical advice; there are no real doctors' testimonials. The illustrations are lively and appealing, the graphics clear and the text easy to read. It is an example of a striking, modern advertisement, successful on many levels. Jubol was variously claimed to cure constipation, migraines, vertigo and enteritis. The manufacturers boasted of supplying the Vatican with their powders. Jubol was a great commercial success and was sold all over Europe.

Cameras and Photography

GEORGE EASTMAN, the founder of the American firm Eastman Kodak, revolutionized photography when, in 1888, he introduced a simple camera with the slogan 'You pull the string, we do the rest'. Kodak would process the film and reload the camera. No longer did the amateur photographer need a darkroom or a knowledge of chemicals. Within five months 2,500 cameras had been sold, and within a few years Kodak had become the largest photographic business in the world.

In the Ensign advertisement, Britishness is stressed in picture and copy. A young woman snaps her fiancé or brother in naval uniform, a bulldog at his feet. In the background an Army officer chats to another young woman. Britishness is to be expected in a wartime advertisement, yet the image of a woman using a camera, designed to show that anyone could take a photograph, stems from the 'Kodak Girl' campaign of 1901. The 'Kodak Girl' lasted for many years, her fashions changing as the years passed. Ensign's advertisement was even drawn by the same artist, Fred Pegram, who had drawn the 1914 British 'Kodak Girl'.

Ensign cameras cost 10 shillings (50p), but the cheapest Kodak cost 30 shillings (£1.50) in 1914, so

Sphere, 27 July 1918, p. ii

the Ensign was a bargain. There was always the possibility that one's fiancé might not return from the war, and a photograph might be all that one had to remember him by. Ensign cameras were good, but Kodak was larger, and had more technical expertise and more money for research and marketing. George Eastman knew what people wanted before they realized they wanted it. As he put it, 'The public has to be educated to its own needs.'

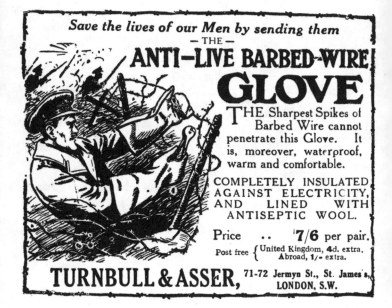

Save the lives of our Men by sending them
— THE —
ANTI—LIVE BARBED-WIRE
GLOVE

THE Sharpest Spikes of Barbed Wire cannot penetrate this Glove. It is, moreover, waterproof, warm and comfortable.

COMPLETELY INSULATED AGAINST ELECTRICITY, AND LINED WITH ANTISEPTIC WOOL.

Price .. '7/6 per pair.

Post free { United Kingdom, 4d. extra. Abroad, 1/- extra.

TURNBULL & ASSER, 71-72 Jermyn St., St. James's, LONDON, S.W.

Military Gadgets

IN *Memoirs of an Infantry Officer*, Siegfried Sassoon, then a second lieutenant, told how he went to the Army & Navy Stores to buy two pairs of wire-cutters and a pistol. Gadgets by the score were on offer in the Weapon Department. The assistant tried to persuade Sassoon to buy a periscope, but he wanted neither periscope nor the patent earplugs which were also on display. Barbed wire was the problem, and the cutters which had been issued to his company were blunt. It was not the German wire that Sassoon wished to cut. Gaps had to be made in the British wire before an attack, so that he and his men could reach the German trenches. Barbed wire, invented to stop cattle from straying, had first been used in the American Civil War of 1861–65, and became a defining feature of trench warfare in France and Flanders. Belts of wire between 10 and 30 yards (10–30 metres) deep were usually enough to make the enemy's life difficult. It was very rare for wire to be electrified, but it did happen sometimes in Belgium where mains electricity was available. Lieutenant Freyberg, of the Royal Naval Division, was leading his men out of Antwerp in October 1914, with the Germans close behind. He grasped some barbed wire, and found that the Belgians had electrified it. It was some time before the 'off' switch could be found, and his electrically clenched muscles released from the wire.

Many advertisements used variations on the phrase 'Send a Tin to Your Soldier Friend', appealing to relatives and fiancées, rather than the men themselves. Rat-traps ('Germany's Allies – Rats'), trench-bayonets, collapsible megaphones and body armour were just some of the gadgets on offer. Body armour sounds good in theory, but the practice was different. In *Soldier from the Wars Returning* Captain Charles Carrington wrote that one of his friends had been killed in July 1916 when a piece of shrapnel struck his steel breastplate and drove a steel splinter into his lungs. Steel breastplates were too cumbersome to wear all the time. Carrington said that soldiers only thought about gadgets when they were in a quiet sector of the line. In battle, they thought about essentials. The regulation steel helmets, first issued experimentally in the winter of 1915–16, were far more popular. Not only did they offer protection from shrapnel, but the broad brim kept off the rain. They could also be used as candlesticks, washing bowls or pillows. Second Lieutenant Robert Graves, who spent much of the war in the same battalion as Siegfried Sassoon, began his front-line career decked out like a Christmas tree, as soldiers used to say. He carried a revolver, field glasses, wire-cutters, a flask of whisky, a periscope and a compass. When he returned to the front line as a captain in January 1917 after he had recovered from his wounds, he

Dont put your fingers in your ears

GUN DEAFNESS is much more easily and effectively prevented by the use of **HARBUTT'S**

Fibrous PLASTICINE

A small piece made into plugs placed in the ears cuts up the nerve shattering concussions of gun fire in Battery action, and the intense crashing of incessantly bursting shells.

Strong tin pocket cases, 7d. and 1/2 post paid. Extra if sent to the Expeditionary Forces—3d. on the small box, and 9d. on the large.

HARBUTT'S PLASTICINE, Ltd.

50 Bathampton, BATH.

"AN ABSOLUTE NECESSITY for the GUNNERS."

Minimise the Risk

Many of the casualties caused by shrapnel, bayonet, spent bullets and splinters could be prevented by wearing the 'Crossman Body Shield.'

It is made from the same class steel as the helmets which have proved so valuable in saving life. It is constructed to fit the body for the purpose of deflecting rifle and machine gun fire.

The 'CROSSMAN'

(HUNT'S PATENT)

BODY SHIELD

Adjustable, weight almost imperceptible, no restriction or discomfort to wearer. Covered khaki twill. The top and bottom edges are constructed with a slightly outward curve to prevent bayonet thrusts from glancing off the shield either up or down.

£2.2.0   *Packed Free and Carriage Paid to any address at Home or Abroad.*

TYLER & TYLER, Halford House, Leicester.
Agents can be appointed.

Bystander, 2 August 1916, p. 216

took only a pair of wire-cutters and an electric torch. He had discarded his pistol in favour of a rifle. A man who was not carrying a rifle was obviously an officer, and was a target for German snipers.

The noise of an artillery barrage, whether one was firing the guns or being shelled, was deafening. Nothing like it had ever been heard before. Some compared the noise of a single shell arriving to the passing of an express train. British soldiers would say that Jerry was 'sending over iron foundries'. Germans described a heavy barrage as *'Trommel-feuer'*, drum-fire. Soldiers were, as ever, expected to endure. Harbutt's were enterprising in promoting Plasticine® as earplugs. Plasticine had been invented in the late 1890s by William Harbutt, an art teacher who wanted his students to have modelling clay that could be endlessly reworked without setting hard. It was soon marketed as a children's toy.

The Royal Flying Corps, a branch of the army, went to France in 1914 with 109 officers and 66 aeroplanes. In May 1918, the newly formed Royal Air Force had 1,658 pilots and 1,260 serviceable aircraft. The RFC and the Royal Naval Air Service 'spotted' fall of shot for the artillery, photographed German trenches, and tried to prevent the Germans from doing the same. In 1918, they began long-range strategic bombing. The rapid expansion of the RFC and the RNAS encouraged technical innovation. Aircraft could go faster, climb higher and man-oeuvre more quickly by 1918, but they still had open cockpits, and it was very cold at 20,000 feet (6,000

Suits
Aviation

The 'Air-Velope'

Built up on entirely new scientific lines, the details of which we shall make known shortly.

—◆—

Positively cold, wind, and wet proof.

—◆—

As sketch, with fur collar,

£10 : 10 : 0

ROBINSON & CLEAVER LTD.

Naval and Military Outfitters,
156-168 Regent St.,
LONDON,
W.1.

Land and Water, 11 April 1918, p. xi

metres). Robinson & Cleaver's suit, advertised in
April 1918 – the month that the RFC became the
RAF – symbolizes the change in aerial warfare that
had taken place since August 1914, when pilots had
flown at lower altitudes, wearing little more than
their uniform and a leather jacket.

WILL YOU HELP OUR ALLIES?

EACH nation is fighting valiantly, but France has provided the battlefield, resulting in untold loss, direct and indirect, to her people and industries.

YOU can help her sick and wounded soldiers enormously by sending a cheque to the French Ambassador or the Hon. Treasurer, and gifts in kind to the Hon. Secretary,

CROIX ROUGE FRANÇAISE

Comité de Londres:

9, KNIGHTSBRIDGE, S.W.

Patrons :   H.M. Queen Alexandra.
            H.E. Paul Cambon, French Ambassador.
Présidente - - -   Vicomtesse de la Panouse.
Hon. Auditors - -   Price, Waterhouse & Co.

Punch, 14 April 1915, p. ix

Charitable Appeals

❖⸺◉◉⸺❖

WHEN THE German army crossed the Belgian frontier on 4 August 1914, it brought with it artillery of a size and power that had never before been used in Western Europe. It also brought eight cavalry divisions, the largest body of horsemen ever assembled in Western Europe. Heavy artillery could destroy cities and kill or wound men and horses more horribly then ever before, yet armies were Napoleonic in their dependence on the horse, and unarmoured infantrymen were still needed to fight battles. The tank was in the future. Horses were used as cavalry, and for hauling field guns and transport wagons. In 1914 the German army mobilized 715,000 horses, the British army 165,000 and the Russian army over a million. Men and horses all needed feeding, watering and looking after when they were wounded.

The Red Cross had been founded in 1863 as an international humanitarian organization. During the war it provided doctors, ambulances, stretcher-bearers, orderlies and a huge army of volunteer nurses – the VADs, middle- and upper-class young women such as Vera Brittain without whose help the Royal Army Medical Corps would have been overwhelmed (see *Nursing Equipment*). Despite the hard-working, unpaid duchesses, countesses and debutantes, the organization could not function without money, and the British, French, Italian and Russian Red Cross committees appealed for funds regularly throughout the war.

Countless soldiers spoke of the food, cups of tea and cheering words which they had received in the front line from the YMCA and the Salvation Army. One young soldier had been greeted by a female Salvation Army adjutant with the words 'Now, lad, you look tired. I am going to make you an extra strong cup of tea.' The soldier burst into tears, and said that he had thought that no one cared whether he lived or died. Another soldier said that, even if he lived to be a hundred, he would never forget the breakfast that the Salvation Army had cooked for him at four a.m. on a cold morning, when he had not eaten for thirty-six hours. 'It is never too early or too late to help a soldier', as one Salvationist said (Adjutant Mary Booth, *With the BEF in France*).

The Church Army had been founded by the Reverend Wilson Carlile in 1882, four years after the Salvation Army. Carlile, a curate, felt that the Church of England was out of touch and needed a practical, evangelical branch. In 1904 King Edward VII asked General William Booth, the Salvation Army's founder, what the established churches thought of him. 'Sir, they imitate me', Booth replied. The Church Army did good work, but it was part of the established Church and would never be able to compete with the Salvationists, who were fired by an evangelical, Nonconformist fervour. The Salvation Army had developed its muscles

Punch, 26 December 1917, back cover

by sending working-class officers, as it called its ministers, into working-class districts and by giving female officers the responsibility for helping girls and women who had been driven into prostitution. Women were more equal in the Salvation Army than in any other religious organization. The Salvation Army fed soldiers, provided ambulances, looked after soldiers' families and traced missing persons. 'It exists for one purpose only, to do good', as an advertisement in the *Graphic* said in 1917.

The wounded cavalryman in the RSPCA advertisement must have had some success, for a German *Pickelhaube* hangs from his bedhead. The advertisement says 'No army can fight without horses'. In 1916 this was true, although the cavalry was no longer the most important mounted arm. The horses the army relied on were those of the Royal Horse Artillery and the draught horses of the Royal Army Service Corps, which hauled transport wagons. Although British cavalrymen had also been trained to fight as mounted mobile infantry and were armed with Lee-Enfield rifles, there were cavalry charges as late as October 1918 when the German army was retreating, and the Canadian cavalry had captured four hundred men and almost a hundred machine guns at Cambrai in November 1917. The Great War was the cavalry's last hurrah, and no one could begrudge the motor ambulances, in effect luxury horseboxes, built for the RSPCA and the Blue Cross by coachbuilders who had made bodies for Rolls-Royce and Daimler cars in peacetime.

Footlights "At the Front"

WHAT they need is entertainment. The "Decca" is Theatre, Music Hall, and Concert Room in one. Looking just like a hand-bag when closed, when open it is as powerful and as rich in tone, and as clear in reproduction as expensive Cabinet Gramophones. Strongly made to stand the hard knocks of Active Service use. Weighs only about 13 lbs., and plays all makes and sizes of needle records.

THE DECCA
DULCEPHONE

The Portable Gramophone

In 3 Styles.

| Leather-Cloth Case, **£2 10 0** | Compressed Fibre, **£3 10 0** | Solid Cowhide, **£5 15 0** |

Of HARRODS, ARMY & NAVY STORES, WHITELEY'S, and all leading Stores and Music Dealers. Descriptive pamphlet with name of nearest agent free on application to the Manufacturers :—

THE DULCEPHONE CO.,
32–36 Worship St., London, E.C.

"They" shall have music wherever they go.

Land and Water, 10 July 1915, p. 247

Gramophones

G RAMOPHONES HAD been widely available since
the late 1890s. Decca developed the world's first
portable gramophone in 1912. The shellac records,
which revolved at 78 r.p.m., lasted for a maximum of
three minutes. The life of a soldier on the Western
Front was not unrelentingly miserable. Troops
spent an average of only eight days in the front-line
trenches before they were relieved. Battles were not
continuous. There were quiet sectors of the front
where nothing happened for months, even though
the Germans were only yards away. Soldiers sometimes got seven days' leave – long enough to see a
West End musical whose pretty girls and jolly songs
would divert their minds from the war. They could
take records of their favourite songs, such as 'Take
Me Back to Dear Old Blighty', back to their dug-
outs and play them on a clockwork gramophone.
The gramophone needed no electricity; its acoustic
amplifier worked by vibration. Gramophones soon
became an indispensable part of life in dug-outs,
YMCA recreation huts and hospitals. In February
1916 an officer in charge of a hospital wrote to *The
Times*: 'Only those who live and work among the
nerve-shattered wounded can appreciate the joy of
the gramophone to the patients whose brains are

teeming with the screech of shells and the noise of bombs.'

Judging by the date of the newspaper cutting of 5 April 1918 which is used in the *Tatler* advertisement, the young officer whose gramophone has been stolen by the 'Cussed Huns' was in the front line on 21 March 1918 when the Germans attacked on the Somme. This was Operation Michael, one of the last major German attacks of the war. Some 7,000 British infantrymen had been killed and 21,000 captured in one day. The officer was lucky in that the Huns had got his gramophone, rather than him.

"The cussed Huns have got my gramophone"

to the Army Pay Corps

Another Loss Made Good.

The other day I quoted from the letter of a young officer who, referring to the loss of personal belongings owing to the German onrush, said, "worst of all, the cussed Huns have got my gramophone." The note has touched the heart of one of my readers, who has written asking me for the address of the officer, so that he may send him a new gramophone.

A small incident, but typical of the spirit of the nation—anxiety to make every loss good.

Another reader says "Your note re the officer's loss of a gramophone is rather interesting, as my own son (captain, R. F.) wrote on the 24th : Of course, we have certainly lost a lot of guns and stores of all kinds (possibly a gramophone !).' They do think a lot of their music ! "

Seeing that two out of every three gramophones at the front are "Deccas," the chances are that the one mentioned in the Evening Standard, April 5th, was a "Decca."

THE "Decca" is the ideal gramophone for Active Service. It can be carried with ease anywhere. No case required ; no loose parts to get lost. Plays perfectly all makes and sizes of needle records.

THE DECCA

THE PORTABLE GRAMOPHONE

In Leather Cloth. £6 15 0	Compressed Fibre, £7 17 6	Solid Cowhide £10 10 0

Of Harrods, Army and Navy Stores, Whiteley's, Selfridge's, Gamage's, and all leading Stores and Music Dealers. ILLUSTRATED FOLDER, and name of nearest agent, free on application to the Manufacturers—

THE DULCEPHONE CO., 36, WORSHIP ST., LONDON, E.C. 2.

(Proprietors : BARNETT SAMUEL & SONS, Ltd.)

Tatler, 22 May 1918, p. 223

PETER ROBINSON'S

Opening Showing of this Season's Corsetry
Featuring ROYAL WORCESTER Corsets with the

NEW MILITARY CURVE

The smart new Military vogue of this Autumn calls for an important change in corset styles, and infinite care taken in the selection of our new models. Ladies may therefore place absolute reliance upon the latest Royal Worcester Kidfitting Corsets we are introducing at this Exhibit being correct in style and of the greatest possible value.

A number of particularly clever Royal Worcester Kidfitting Corsets with the New Military Curve — which gives the Erect Poise without any discomfort — are confined exclusively to us. Our stock of Royal Worcester Corsets is always the largest in England; but present conditions make it so difficult for such high-grade Corsets to be produced in anything like sufficient quantities to meet the demand, that ladies desiring all the advantages of a full choice of styles are asked to call or write for a selection on approval at once, as there is likely to be a delay of some weeks before our stock, once sold, can be replenished.

EXPERT FITTERS IN ATTENDANCE.

ROYAL WORCESTER
Kidfitting Corsets.

MODEL 8520.

For the medium figure with full bust and slight hip. Has a radically new feature in the fan-shaped bust gore. 6 hose-supporters. Sizes 20 - 30 ins. In white coutil. Price 21/-

Catalogue post free.

PETER ROBINSON, LTD., OXFORD ST., LONDON, W.

Ladies' Fashions

❖═◗ ◖═❖

T HE FIRST WORLD WAR caused a revolution in dress for women. Fashion had its dictates, but for once practicality took the lead. As the role of women in society developed and changed, women's clothing, underwear as well as outerwear, had to change drastically.

There were still remnants of restrictive Victorian corsetry and skirt design in 1914. In many ways Edwardian dress shapes were equally 'hobbling'. The New Military Curve Corset sold by Peter Robinson in 1915 is typical, promoting the classic Edwardian silhouette with a large, low bust and tiny waist and hips. The skirt worn over this would have been extremely narrow and close fitting, as would the jacket or blouse. Freedom of movement would have been impossible.

New flexible, elasticized materials were replacing steel and whaleboned corsets, however, and shorter corsets with separate *soutien-gorge* – a French euphemism for chest support – or brassieres were becoming popular in France. In 1913 Wick's designed a 'sports' corset, resembling a girdle. Before the war it was described as suitable for dancing the tango; in 1914 it was deemed appropriate for nurses and VADs. Work was bringing women freedom in more ways than one.

The earliest uniforms for women war-workers, that of the Red Cross for example, were old-fashioned, full length, slim-fitting and tailored. They would have required great efforts in laundering and pressing to keep them in good condition. Attitudes and silhouettes were softening as the conflict pro-gressed. In March 1915 the Board of Trade set up the Register of Women for War Service, exhorting the female population to take up 'paid employment of any kind – industrial, agricultural, clerical'. Remuneration was not always generous. One pound a week was a typical wage for a young woman in an unskilled occupation. It was quite acceptable in 1915 for a woman to be paid half the amount a man would have received, when replacing him in the workforce. There was resistance to women replacing men in some industries. Glasgow was the first city to train women as tram conductors and drivers; the ladies sported smart, long tartan skirts and plain jackets. In Coventry men refused to train women to run trams and threatened strike action if they were given permanent jobs.

In the spring of 1915 it became obvious that agricultural labour shortages might cause a crisis. Farmers suggested that young boys should be excused school to assist with milking and care of horses. Women were not welcome as agricultural workers. This changed as manpower decreased further. Over the course of the war a quarter of a million women worked on the land, ploughing, milking and digging. Many were young women who

The R.F.C. GIRL

The
"R.F.C." GIRL
knows by experience that to
keep out the wet and for comfort
in any sort of bad weather
there is nothing to equal a
"CRAVENETTE" SHOWERPROOF.

Cravenette
(Regd)

IDEAL for ALL
OUTDOOR WEAR.
If any difficulty in obtaining, please write
The Cravenette Co., Ltd.,
(Dept. 17), Well Street,
Bradford.

No Guarantee
without this Stamp:

REGD TRADE MARK
Cravenette
PROOFED BY
The Cravenette Co Ltd

Tatler, 19 June 1918, p. iv

'DRI - GARB' OUTFIT

LIGHT, comfortable, tough and weatherproof, this "Dri-garb" Outfit is "the right thing." It is attractive, practical, "trustworthy" and splendidly economical.

*Postal Orders
Carefully
Executed.*

*Carriage Paid
in the U.K.*

'Dri - Garb'
Out.it
in fine Twill

Coat ...	25/9
Breeches	13/9
(Laced at knee.)	
Leggings	8/11
Hat ...	4/11

(Special Orders
5/- extra.)

SUNBONNETS, in
Khaki only,
N9½ 3/6

R. I. 300.—Farmers' Smock of good Khaki Jean. Summer weight, excellentl· made and finished. Detachable buttons. Women's Size, 4/11. Outsize, 5/6.

HARRODS Ld Richard Burbidge Managing Director LONDON S W

Land and Water, 17 May 1917, p. 26

had a refreshing and pragmatic approach to dress. According to journalist Dorothy Peel, the land girls 'with their bobbed heads, breeches, thick boots and smocks at first shocked the sensibilities and then captured the affections of the country folk'.

The Harrods Dri-Garb advertisements from May 1917 show the genesis of twentieth-century female workwear in the war years. Hemlines have risen 4 inches (10 cm); smocks, overalls and jackets are loosely fitted. Shoes and boots are sturdy and comfortable. There is no sign of a corset or a floor-length petticoat. Fabrics are tough but breathable. Thomas Burberry and the visionaries of the rational dress movement have succeeded at last. Women have introduced a new way of dressing, shaped by real bodies and their independent lives and experiences.

The unisex trend, first seen most obviously in ladies' trench-coat design, continued unabated during the war. The Cravenette showerproof of 1918 fulfils a role somewhere between uniform and practical dress. The coat has broad shoulders, loose-fitting sleeves and a relaxed, belted waist, resembling a man's coat. The 'hourglass' shape has disappeared. This advertisement was published in the *Tatler*; the one next to it showed the latest in ladies' combinations from Gorringe's. Fine knitted with no stays, the combinations comprised an all-in-one vest and knee-length long johns – perfect unrestricted underwear suitable for any occupation and again copied from male designs and customized for a natural, female shape.

Fashion in general mimicked the changes seen most clearly in workwear. Day dresses, tea dresses and evening gowns had become simpler, un-structured and almost trimming-free. One dress might even do duty for all three times of day. Tea frocks were particularly popular, designed for the modern woman and suitable for home, dinner or restaurant wear. Department stores such as Selfridge's and Marshall & Snelgrove advertised widely in newspapers and magazines, offering fashion advice at a time when socially acceptable standards in dress were changing at a bewildering speed. The *Tatler* and the recently launched *Vogue* – autumn 1916 – emphasized the importance of dressing 'correctly'.

There was still a place for luxury fabrics and frivolous ruffles and lace – often under the practical tea dress or plain twill uniform. Venn's 'unlimited dainty undies' were advertised widely in magazines read by men and women. Cheeky rhymes featured lovely girls doing war work, who enjoy 'exquisite, filmy, lacy things' in their time off. This lingerie is unstructured and alluring. Passion is hinted at in a Venn's advertisement from 1917 in the *Tatler*, with one minimally clad lady resting her foot on a tiger-skin rug – a powerful image of a New Woman in modern dress.

VENN'S Undies

If Not—Why Not?

Call in at our New Premises at

14–15, Conduit St., W. 1

or 'phone for a selection of our Dainty Undies to be sent to you. Mayfair 1407.

Violet Velma Vere de Vere
  Was a dainty, delicious, delicate dear ;
Delightfully dressed from top to toe,
For she always ' got it at VENN'S, you know ! "

Exquisite, filmy, lacey things,
  (My imagination, you see, has wings !)
Were Violet's dearest dream of delight
By day and—whisper it gently !—night.

Now the very last thing you'd have thought she'd do
  Was to work "on the land." But she did ! It's true !
For she couldn't nurse and she wouldn't knit,
But was awfully keen on " doing her bit."

Never a day but she rakes and digs,
  And plants potatoes and feeds the pigs . . .
But doesn't she just enjoy her Sundays,
When she revels again in her dainty "undies" !

You should write for our new "Thumb Book," which will amuse and please you.

Exquisite Lacey Crêpe Chemise and Knickers, as sketch, £2 12 6. In Ivory, Black, Champagne, and Helio only.

Tatler, 2 May 1917, p. vii

Pity she didn't send me an Onoto.

The pen which needs no filler is the only pen for your Soldier Friend.

Send him a Military size Onoto, the pen which fills itself in a flash from any ink supply, and carries safely in any position in the uniform pocket.

The Onoto never leaks.

An interesting letter from F. J. F., 9th Middlesex Regt., Dinapore, Behar, India.

"The Onoto Pen has been with me ever since I left home, banged about in my kit-bag, in all sorts of positions, and has never leaked, it has been filled with various inks and has never clogged, and no part has gone wrong, which is an important point out here where it would be very difficult to get a pen repaired. Another outstanding feature is that while other fellows' pens have been put out of action owing to broken fillers, this one is self-filling, and therefore safer for rough usage."

Onoto
THE Pen

Needs no Filler.

FROM 10/6

THOMAS DE LA RUE & CO., LTD.

Actual size

Fountain Pens

WINSTON CHURCHILL resigned from the Cabinet on 11 November 1915. He had been a reserve officer ever since he left the army in 1899. Soldiering, which he loved, would be an escape from political failure. On 20 November, he went to France as a major, attached to the 2nd Battalion Grenadier Guards, in the front line at Neuve Chapelle. Churchill wrote to his wife Clementine almost every day. His letters are a mixture of affection for Clementine and the children, descriptions of life in the trenches, and lists of kit which he asked Clementine to buy for him. On 21 November he asked for a sleeping bag, trench waders, and a periscope, 'most important'. Two days later he asked for a new Onoto fountain pen, as he had lost his own. Churchill continued writing to his wife for the rest of his six-month stint in the trenches. He told her that he loved her, and that he kissed her photograph every night. He thanked her for the 'divine and glorious' sleeping bag, and said that the periscope was the exact type that he wanted. One wonders if he could see German snipers as clearly as the lieutenant in the Lifeguard Periscope advertisement shown on page 11.

The postal service was good. In large British cities there were five or more collections and deliveries each day, with a delivery on Sundays. All post for the Western Front was sorted at the London Home Depot, a temporary sorting office in Regent's Park. By the end of the war, over 2 billion letters and 114 million parcels had passed through the depot. The Swan advertisement shows how powerful a pen could be, as the troops fire off their 5 million letters a week. A letter was the only means of reassuring one's family, expressing affection, and asking for the things which made life on the front line more bearable.

Despite the cost (10 shillings and sixpence, or 52½p, was nearly eleven days' basic pay for an infantry private), Swan, Onoto and Waterman advertisements all show ordinary soldiers using fountain pens, or wishing for them. The advertisements are all aimed at friends or relatives who would like more letters 'from your friend on active service', and two were published in late November, with Christmas presents in mind.

It seems strange now to imagine soldiers using fountain pens in dugouts, or captured pillboxes, and it is difficult to know how common these pens really were in the trenches. Despite the best efforts of advertisers, many soldiers wrote their letters in pencil.

Corporal Reginald McCarthy, of the 6th East Yorkshire Regiment, wrote his notebook in the front line at Passchendaele in 1917. The platoon roll of

The Graphic, 25 November 1916, p. 670

5,000,000 letters a week

The Postmaster-General recently stated that the letters sent home by our fighting men amount to 5,000,000 letters a week.

THE "SWAN" FOUNT PEN

Sends letters from the front

Safety Pattern from 12/6

Standard Pattern from 10/6

and plays a big part in producing this colossal mail bag. The "Swan" is just the pen for fighting men. Quick and easy to use. No internal mechanism and no perishable parts. Unaffected by climatic conditions. Takes "Swan" Ink Tablets when fluid ink is unobtainable. If you are not getting as many letters as you would like from your friend on Active Service, don't blame him. Send him a "Swan." You've no idea how it helps.

fifty-seven men is in neat copperplate handwriting, in fountain pen, as are the instructions for using a Lewis gun. Second Lieutenant Charles Carrington had to censor his men's letters. All had left school at the age of 12, but the standard of English was high, even if some of the writing was formal: 'I now take pen in hand to write this, hoping it finds you in the pink as it leaves me at present.' When time was short, or officers were unable to censor letters, field postcards were used. These had phrases such as 'I am quite well', 'I have been admitted into hospital' and 'I am being sent down to the base' already printed on them. The writer struck out the un-wanted words, signed the card and posted it. There was a warning at the top of the card: 'If anything else is added the post card will be destroyed.'

Royal Vinolia
Vanishing Cream

BEAUTY *on* DUTY *has a* DUTY TO BEAUTY

For the RED CROSS WORKER.

THE arduous duties of the Red Cross worker do not leave her much time to devote to the care of her skin and complexion. Royal Vinolia Vanishing Cream is all that is needed. Royal Vinolia Vanishing Cream is the most convenient of preparations for the war worker; it can be applied in a moment.

A little of this delightful and soothing cream rubbed on the skin regularly will prevent it from being roughened by inclement weather, give the complexion a clear, healthy bloom, and keep the hands soft and white.

To all workers in the open, **Royal Vinolia Talcum Powder** *is a necessity. It absorbs perspiration and protects the skin from the effects of wind and sun; delicately perfumed.* **Tins, 10d. & 1/3.**

Royal Vinolia Vanishing Cream. In Tubes, 7½d. & 1/- Pots, 1/-

VINOLIA COMPANY LTD., LONDON—PARIS.
R V 337—34

Soap and Skin Cream

❖═◉═❖

SOME OF THE most appealing and evocative advertisements published during the First World War were created to encourage women to buy soap or face cream. Vinolia produced a striking set of advertisements showing women in action as Red Cross drivers, operating lathes, working a plough. A lovely young woman is holding a spanner against the background of a smoking factory. The message is simple: vanishing cream is vital. No matter how women's lives were being revolutionized in terms of work and activity, physical appearance was still of paramount importance. The Vinolia slogan sums it up: 'Beauty on Duty has a Duty to Beauty.'

In August 1918 the back page of *Punch* featured a full-page black-and-white advertisement with a pensive young woman sitting on a clifftop, looking out to sea. She is wearing a chain of flowers – poppies – and she is surrounded by them. The flowers are printed in red, the only vivid colour on the page apart from her wide-brimmed red hat. The advertising copy is titled 'Consolation'. The product? Colleen vanishing cream. In spite of grief and uncertainty a woman's priority in 1918, as always, was to look beautiful.

More women were working than ever at the end of the Great War. An additional 1,800,000 women had joined the workforce and over 80 per cent of munitions were made by women. They had a sizeable disposable income, often for the first time in their lives, and manufacturers of cosmetics vied with each other to devise attractive advertising and products to make them part with it. Pomeroy Skin Food was advertised in the *Tatler* with a vignette showing a 'munitionette' filling a shell case, advising the use of Mrs Pomeroy's preparation to avoid 'the munition complexion'. Reactions to the chemicals in shell cases included severe eczema, jaundice and death. Mrs Pomeroy's cream was unlikely to help.

The manufacturers of Pears soap were on much safer ground. Their translucent, mild soap had been supplied to the gentry since 1789. Its natural ingredients, fragrance and maturing process produced a gentle, hard-wearing soap that perfectly conveyed a message of economy in wartime. Pears had revolutionized advertising in the nineteenth century, using popular paintings including Millais' *Bubbles* to anchor its brand in the popular consciousness. In wartime generic or society beauties featured in their advertising instead, and for the first time the beauties were working: as nurses, land girls or gardeners.

The soldiers at the front were bombarded with advertisements for grooming products; advertisers used a variety of persuasive approaches. Cleanliness was next to hygiene, as well as to godliness. It had a moral connotation as well as a physical one.

PEARS, the soap of ancestral fame. In all the history of commerce no soap has such an inspiring record. Of transparent purity, beautifying the complexion, refreshing to a degree and with a subtle fragrance all its own, PEARS for more than a century has been the chosen soap of the woman of refinement. It is also pre-eminent for its lasting qualities, therefore to

Practise Economy—use

Pears' Soap

The **CLEANEST** fighter in the World—
the British Tommy

The clean, chivalrous fighting instincts of our gallant soldiers reflect the ideals of our business life. The same characteristics which stamp the British Tommy as the *CLEANEST FIGHTER IN THE WORLD* have won equal repute for British Goods.

SUNLIGHT SOAP

is typically British. It is acknowledged by experts to represent the highest standard of Soap Quality and Efficiency. Tommy welcomes it in the trenches just as you welcome it at home.

£1,000 GUARANTEE OF PURITY ON EVERY BAR.

The name Lever on Soap is a Guarantee of Purity and Excellence.

LEVER BROTHERS LIMITED, PORT SUNLIGHT.

Land and Water, 4 September 1915, back cover

Lifebuoy soap purported to protect soldiers from typhoid, cholera and infectious diseases. May Queen powdered toilet soap 'instantly cured sore and tired feet'. Smartly brilliantined hair and a well-shaved chin were essential to maintaining an officer's dignity and morale in general. Sunlight and Wright's Coal Tar Soap were affordable for all ranks, supplying 'the cleanest fighters in the world', and remained enormous sellers until the 1960s, embedded in the nation's heart – another huge success for Lever Bros, owners of the Pears brand. Cleanliness was a small sign of control over the chaos of war.

Land and Water, 18 December 1915, p. 624

Military Outfitters

B ETWEEN THE outbreak of war in August 1914 and the Armistice in 1918, 247,061 officers were commissioned into the army. This created a lucrative market for military tailors, whose advertisements appeared in newspapers and magazines ranging from *The Times* to *Punch* and the *Tatler*. 'Other ranks' were issued with kit, but officers were given an allowance – £50 in February 1915 – and had to buy their own. Thresher & Glenny's advertisements were aimed at new officers who knew little of military life. The advertisements stressed the hundred-year history of the firm, the distinction of its clients and the moderate charges. Second Lieutenant Charles Carrington said that his £50 allowance easily covered sword, revolver, two service-dress uniforms, great-coat and all the accessories. The advertisement on page 84, of an officer in tropical kit and sola topi, is a reminder that British and Imperial forces were fighting in the Middle East and Africa as well as on the Western Front.

There were rules, both official and unofficial, about the cut, colour and detail of officers' uniform. Newly gazetted officers, especially those who did not come from army families, encountered many unforeseen problems. Second Lieutenant Siegfried Sassoon was fortunate, in that a friend had recommended his own military tailor. Sassoon was welcomed when he joined his regiment, but the adjutant was appalled by the cut of another new officer's jacket, and by the yellow tinge of his shirt and tie. Many of the new officers were 'temporary gentlemen', whose education and background were very different from those of most officers of the regular army. As the war progressed, and casualties mounted, no one cared any more if an officer had not been to public school, or spoke broad Lancashire, so long as he was a good officer. Of the 144,075 officers demobilized by May 1920, 1,016 had been miners in 1914.

Tailors worked hard to win customers. Burberry, who supplied uniforms as well as trench coats, had a branch in Paris and agents in towns in France and Flanders. Officers could go on leave to towns behind the lines where life was still relatively normal, have a haircut and a proper bath, and do their shopping. Captain F.C. Hitchcock said that in Poperinghe he found shops that sold uniforms, caps, South African war medal ribbons, puttees, button-sticks and almost every military accessory a soldier might require. In November 1915 Moss Bros advertised that 'Time saved means longer leave', promising that they could supply a made-to-measure uniform in London in twenty-four hours.

Khaki service dress uniform had been officially introduced in 1902 as a result of experience gained in Imperial wars both large and small. It was practical, comfortable and inconspicuous to the enemy.

KIT

Tatler, 19 December 1917, p. 1

JOINING KITS FOR EVERY BRANCH OF HIS MAJESTY'S SERVICE.

Thresher and Glenny's representative attends by appointment any camp in England for the convenience of Cadets receiving commissions.

MILITARY OUTFITS.

" A firm established as Military Outfitters during the Crimean War and Indian Mutiny, with the outfitting experience of the South African War and the two Egyptian Campaigns well within the memory of many of its staff, is entitled to deal with the subject of Military Outfitting with some degree of authority,"—(" Land & Water," March 23.)

A JOINING KIT.

The following estimate includes all necessary for joining on receiving a first commission : Serge F.S. Jacket, 63s. ; Whipcord ditto, 70s. ; 1 pair Slacks, 25s. ; 1 pair Whipcord Knicker Breeches, 35s. ; Service Cap, 15s. 6d. ; British Warm, 84s. ; Sam Browne Belt, 42s. ; Whistle and Cord, Lanyard, Puttees, 2 Khaki Flannel Shirts and Tie, Stars, Cap, and Collar Badges, and half a dozen Khaki Handkerchiefs ; total, £20.

TROPICAL KIT.

Khaki Washing Drills, Twillettes, Sunproof and Tropical Serges. Drill F.S. Jackets, buttons, etc., detachable, 35s. ; Calvin Cord Riding Breeches, 38s. ; Drill Slacks and Shorts, 16s. 6d. and 12s. 6d. ; Wolseley Helmets, 21s. ; Sunproof Tunic Shirts, pockets and shoulder straps, 17s. 6d.

W.O. CAMP KIT.

Officers going into camp will require the folding bedstead, chair, bath, basin, and washstand, etc., etc., painted ; price, £7 10s.

Also the Thresher Bolmat. Particulars on page xv of present issue.

THRESHER & GLENNY,

MILITARY TAILORS,

152 & 153 STRAND, LONDON (MAKERS OF THE THRESHER TRENCH COAT)

Nevertheless, warfare was changing rapidly, and further official alterations to the uniform were not welcomed by all regimental colonels. In 1914 officers wore their badges of rank on their cuffs, as may be seen in the Bond of Union advertisement on page 102 and the Lifeguard Periscope advertisement on page 11. These distinctive markings, plus the officers' Sam Browne belts and use of a revolver rather than a rifle, made it easy for German snipers to identify British officers at a distance. Orders were issued that badges of rank were to be transferred to officers' epaulettes. Second Lieutenant Robert Graves arrived at his new regiment wearing the new style of epaulette. The colonel told him that he was not going to have any of his officers wearing a 'wind-up' tunic, and ordered him to report to the regimental tailor at once to have the old-style insignia fitted. Better to die dressed like an officer than to survive by looking drab. *Punch* published a cartoon on 10 March 1915 drawn by Captain Duncan Campbell. It showed an officer in three guises, the first as the military tailor imagined him, the second when setting out for the front, and the third after three weeks in the trenches. The third drawing shows an unshaven, muddy, bedraggled officer wearing a hat similar to the one in the Lincoln Bennett advertisement. He is carrying a rifle rather than a revolver. Pamphlet SS135, 'The Training and Employment of Divisions', issued in January 1918, stated: 'All infantry officers taking part in an attack must be dressed and equipped exactly like the men.' Robert Graves's colonel would not have approved.

Is that tyre made in **your** own country?

Are you a *Practical* patriot, or merely a word-of-mouth one? Do you sport a Union Jack in your coat and American Tyres on your car?

If you are a patriotic Briton—then remember that your country needs every penny that can be spared, to win the war, and especially needs the millions in gold that go out of the Empire every year in the purchase of American Tyres.

Be British—buy British Tyres. Be "Tyre-wise" and buy CLINCHERS —the Best of the British.

CLINCHER

THE FIRST DETACHABLE PNEUMATIC TYRE

ALL PLANTATION RUBBER
MOTOR TYRES.

For Commercial Vehicles fit North British Clincher Solid Rubber Band Tyres.

**THE NORTH BRITISH RUBBER CO., LTD.,
169, Great Portland Street, LONDON, W.**
Factories: Castle Mills. EDINBURGH.

The Practical Patriot

IN 1914 BRITAIN was still the workshop of the world. Manufacture of British brands in the Far East or China to reduce costs was almost unknown, and many firms advertised to remind the public that British alternatives existed to German or even American goods. The USA did not declare war on Germany until April 1917, and until then the makers of Clincher tyres could claim that 'millions in gold' went to the USA every year to pay for tyres without worrying about insulting an ally. Avon also used the patriotic theme, reminding *The Times*'s readers in September 1914 that 'We keep the flag flying at Melksham, where a thousand men of Wiltshire make Avon Tyres', and suggesting that the purchase of German tyres was treasonable. This was an understandable tactic so early in the war, but the Royal Navy's blockade of Germany was so effective that Germany's export trade was seriously damaged, and imports to Germany were restricted. There would have been few, if any, German imports into Britain. When Clincher tyres advertised in *The Times* in November 1915, warning that many German tyres were made in the same factory as Zeppelins, it is likely that they were using this tactic to keep their brand in the eye of the public. The association of

German tyres with Zeppelins, which had killed
and wounded British civilians, would have been
enough to deter many British customers from buying
German tyres, even after the war.

Jesse Boot, a Nottingham herbalist, had realized
in 1877 that his working-class customers were buying
widely advertised patent medicines rather than his
traditional remedies. He transformed his business
by advertising cut-price patent medicines in the
local paper. His weekly takings increased from
£20 to £100. By 1914 Boots the Chemists had 560
shops, and had begun manufacturing medicines on
a large scale. The 1914 *Punch* advertisement is very
well thought out. It catches the reader's eye with a
full-page cartoon, *Punch*-like in tone, and drawn
by Charles Harrison, a regular *Punch* artist. Once
the reader has been hooked, the eye is drawn to the
dense copy on the opposite page where Boots' own
products, 'equal or superior to the German product
replaced', are listed in great detail. No substitute
is suggested for the weeping dachshund which is
following Kaiser Wilhelm to Berlin.

Some patriotic advertising had an unpleasant,
anti-Semitic tone. The catering firm J. Lyons had
been established in 1887 by the Gluckstein brothers,
the British-born sons of Jewish immigrants from
Prussia. In September 1914 Lyons took out advertisements in *The Times*, the *Illustrated London News* and
many other papers to say that they had been granted
a High Court injunction to prevent Lipton's, their
great rivals in the tea business, from suggesting that

THE COOKED-GOOSE STEP.
Grand March-Past of the Not Wanted.

Return to Germany of the Enemy's shop-soiled goods.
(SEE OPPOSITE PAGE.)

Do You Drink German Waters?

APOLLINARIS comes from GERMANY.
PERRIER comes from FRANCE.

The Battle - Cry of the Allies:
"Shoulder to Shoulder, in War and Trade."

Perrier stands as the great representative of France against a host of waters from Germany. Thanks to the iron grip of the British and French Fleets, Perrier is being shipped as usual.

The crowning glory of Perrier is its natural gas, the masterpiece of Nature's Chemistry.

"The Champagne of Table Waters."

London Offices: 45-47, Wigmore St., W.

Perrier mixes perfectly with Whisky, Brandy, or Wines, or with Lemon, Milk, etc. Simply with a slice of lemon Perrier Water is delightful.

N.B.—Perrier is of real value in cases of gout and the uric acid habit generally.

Lyons was owned by Germans. Despite this, Lyons took no chances and announced in October 1914 that they had dismissed all German and Austrian employees, whether naturalized or not.

The 1915 Perrier advertisement says that 'Thanks to the iron grip of the British and French Fleets, Perrier is being shipped as usual'. The Royal Navy kept the sea free of German battleships in 1915, but by 1917 the U-boats of the Kaiserliche Marine had become far more effective, and had sunk so many merchant ships that British food supplies were threatened. It was only the adoption of the convoy system for British merchant ships in April 1917 that brought about a reduction in the number of ships sunk, and the restoration of a reliable food supply. The Royal Navy continued the blockade of German ports throughout the war, and the shortages which this caused helped to bring about the Allied victory, revolution in Germany and the abdication of the Kaiser. When the German armies advanced across the Somme in spring 1918, in one of their final offensives of the war, the troops were astonished when they captured British supply dumps, piled high with goods which had become scarce in their homeland. Colonel Albrecht von Thaer wrote that 'entire divisions totally gorged themselves on food and liquor' and failed to press home their attack.

Garrould's

HOSPITAL NURSES' SALOON.

Complete Equipment of Nurses for Home Detachments and the

SEAT OF WAR.
All Surgical Implements and Appliances in Stock.

Write for Garrould's Catalogue of Nurses' Uniforms, Surgical Instruments and Appliances Post Free.

The "Ideal" Expanding Shoulder Brace.

Scientifically correct in design and principle. Compels deep and correct breathing by straightening the back and correcting round shoulders.

Made in three sizes, small, medium, and large, **4/6** each.

ANTI-GAS-MASK RESPIRATOR.
Chemically charged.
Not injurious.
Ready for immediate use.

It is only necessary to sprinkle the Pad with Water before using. Can be shaped to fit any face.
Price **1/6** each.

SUPPORT BELT.
For General use. In Buff colour. The sides are formed of stout expanding Stockinette edged with elastic. The front and back are made of Sateen Jean. Price **9/6**

The "Canute"
Special Nurses' Watch.
Diameter of Dial, 1⅜ in.
Remarkable value.

In handsomely engraved silver case, with a CROSS in Red enamelled in the centre. Long centre seconds hand, which shows time to one-fifth of a second. Keyless wind. Each one guaranteed. Sent on approval. **21/-**

NURSE POWELL'S OBSTETRIC BINDER.
Made in White Coutil, extra deep, **8/6** each.
N.B.—When ordering, please send normal waist measurement.

E. & R. GARROULD, 150 to 162 Edgware Rd., LONDON, W.

Telegrams : "GARROULD, LONDON."   Telephones : 5320, 5321, & 6297 Paddington.

Nursing Equipment

A T THE outbreak of war in August 1914 there were two main bodies of professional nurses available to the British Army. Both were limited in numbers: the Queen Alexandra Imperial Nursing Service with 463 fully trained nurses and 2,200 reserves; and the Territorial Force Nursing Service, which was 2,783 strong. The British Red Cross and the St John Ambulance had formed the VAD (Voluntary Aid Detachment) organization in 1909 and by the summer of 1914 there were over 2,500 VADs or individual volunteers. By the end of 1914 there were 74,000 VADs, the majority upper- and middle-class women and girls, totally untrained and initially unwelcome in military hospitals.

Many talented women used their own initiative and energy to form conventional and unconventional plans for medical support at home and in the battle zone. The Scottish surgeon and suffragist Elsie Inglis proposed setting up hospitals staffed only by women. The War Office responded: 'My good lady, go home and sit still.' She did not. Dr Inglis established the Scottish Women's Hospitals for Foreign Service. Some nurses took off for Belgium under their own steam. Elsie Knocker, a trained midwife and expert motorcyclist, set up a first-aid post with her friend Mairi Chisholm in the ruined Belgian village of Pervyse. Their bravery was recognized by military decorations from the British and Belgian governments.

Garrould's was one of the major suppliers of uniforms for the War Office, the Red Cross and major hospitals – coats, hats, nurses' aprons, caps and watches, regulation overalls, of a demure, full-length, quasi-Victorian design. The company responded to the needs of nurses and patients and the changing face of warfare. Garrould's also supplied surgical instruments and specialized medical equipment. The Anti Gas Respirator was advertised in July 1915, but does not appear sufficient to offer real protection against lethal gas. The support appliances for pregnant women and 'general use' look more like corsets, restrictive and possibly physically damaging. Wheelchairs were increasingly advertised and Garrould's sold them too, plainly displayed with the rest of their equipment. Allwin's wheelchairs were displayed in context, being used in convalescent homes and on the move. Two women in uniform feature in Allwin's advertisement: a nurse and a tram conductress, reflecting the dramatic changes in the workforce seen every day by the end of the conflict.

Extraordinary advances were made in nursing and medicine during the Great War. Nurses were among the first to prepare saline drips and blood transfusions, which were cutting-edge technology at the beginning of the fighting. By the end of the war these techniques were routinely seen at advance dressing stations, close to where injuries actually occurred. Many British women, including Edith and Florence Stoney, were trained as pioneering radiographers at this time. Madame Curie famously spearheaded the development of the Red Cross radiography units across France. Women's autonomy in the fields of medicine, nursing and science had begun.

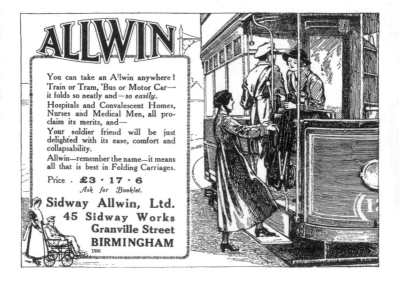

ALLWIN

You can take an Allwin anywhere! Train or Tram, 'Bus or Motor Car— it folds so neatly and—*so easily.*

Hospitals and Convalescent Homes, Nurses and Medical Men, all proclaim its merits, and—

Your soldier friend will be just delighted with its ease, comfort and collapsability.

Allwin—remember the name—it means all that is best in Folding Carriages.

Price . **£3 · 17 · 6**
Ask for Booklet.

Sidway Allwin, Ltd.
45 Sidway Works
Granville Street
BIRMINGHAM

Graphic, 4 May 1918, p. 562

Aiding the Wounded

Never in history has better or more skilful attention been given to the wounded than during the present great war, and the petrol-driven motor ambulance and hospital have given invaluable aid in the great work of mercy. Throughout the war-swept area Red Cross conveyances of the Allied Forces are run upon

"SHELL"
MOTOR SPIRIT

and can therefore be thoroughly depended upon. It is well to remember when purchasing petrol to say 'Shell' and insist upon it. It is supplied for all the services of the Allied Forces only and is obtainable everywhere.

Country Life, 19 December 1914, p. 11

Motor Vehicles

THE BRITISH motor industry had few cars to sell to the public during the war. Everything that they could produce was bought by the armed services. Rolls-Royce were making aero-engines, and Silver Ghost chassis for the War Office and the Admiralty, to be fitted up as armoured cars. Vauxhall were making army staff cars. Daimler were building lorries, ambulances and aero-engines.

When the British Expeditionary Force went to France in August 1914, they took requisitioned lorries with them. Vehicles bearing the names of British railway companies and biscuit manufacturers accompanied the troops through France and Flanders. Fifty London buses, with their drivers, were sent to Antwerp in mid-September to transport Royal Marines, and were soon followed by three hundred more, which carried troops to the First Battle of Ypres. Lieutenant-General Sir Douglas Haig wrote in his diary in September 1914 that horse ambulances were of no use, and that motor ambulances were needed. These went as close to the front line as the state of the roads would allow, and carried the wounded from advanced dressing stations to casualty clearing stations. Shell advertised in *Country Life* in December 1914 that they provided petrol for ambulances, enhancing their reputation by emphasizing their link to a compassionate aspect of the war.

As the Pratt's Motor Spirit advertisement said, it was a petrol war, and vehicles had to be kept running in the field. Daimler built mobile workshops on 3-ton lorry chassis. These were fitted with a lathe, vices, grinder, drill and a forge, and were accompanied by stores vans filled with spares.

The industry had developed rapidly since the repeal of the Locomotive Acts, better known as the Red Flag Acts, in 1896. Until then, three men had to be employed to drive any motor vehicle, and a fourth had to walk in front holding a red flag. Despite the repeal of the Acts, motoring was still seen as a messy and pointless hobby for eccentrics. Few imagined that the car would replace the horse. Alfred Harmsworth, owner of the *Daily Mail*, and an enthusiastic motorist, helped to change the popular view. In 1900 he backed a 1,000-mile reliability trial from London to Edinburgh and back. Sixty-four cars started the run, and forty-seven completed it. By 1914 cars had become a reliable, accepted form of transport. The first Rolls-Royce Silver Ghost had been made in 1906. Alfred Harmsworth, a friend of Rolls-Royce's managing director, Claude Johnson, had suggested the slogan 'The Best Car in the World'. The engineering was superb, but the industry was a large-scale craft process, rather than one organized for mass production. Large numbers of skilled men were needed, which caused problems when war broke out. Men joined up and had to

The DECIDING FACTORS

THIS is a petrol War, Petrol and heavy artillery, according to the consensus of expert military opinion, are to be the deciding factors in the present struggle for supremacy. Speed of transport —of guns and supplies—of men and of food—speed and weight shall prove the winning weapons.

PRATT'S
MOTOR SPIRIT

is used more than any other motor fuel by our own and our Allies' Forces, on land and on sea, in operations at the front.

By Royal   *Appointment.*

THE
ANGLO - AMERICAN OIL CO., LTD.,
Queen Anne's Gate,
LONDON,
S.W.

*My post-war selection,
the "Arrol-Johnston" car.*

Arrol-Johnston, Ld.,

DUMFRIES.

be replaced, often by women who had to be taught engineering skills.

Some advertisers reminded customers that their firms still existed, but were busy with war work. Others stressed that their vehicles were rugged enough to operate on the front line. Arrol-Johnston's advertisements presented a seductive vision of post-war motoring, but the firm did not prosper, and production ended in 1931. A few manufacturers laid the foundations of their post-war success. In 1915 Rolls-Royce built their first aero-engine, the Eagle, based on the engine of the Silver Ghost. Sir Henry Royce had been an apprentice with the Great Northern Railway. He insisted on the highest standards – 'The quality remains long after the price is forgotten.' W.O. Bentley, another ex-GNR apprentice, contributed to the design of the Rolls-Royce Eagle. Bentley had been importing and racing French DFP cars and, thanks to this, he realized that his experience with lightweight aluminium pistons might be useful. He approached the Royal Naval Air Service, which commissioned him as a lieutenant, with a brief to advise on aero-engine manufacture. Bentley persuaded Rolls-Royce to fit aluminium pistons, and went on to design the BR1 and BR2 rotary engines that powered the Sopwith Camel and Snipe. In 1919 the prototype 3-litre Bentley car was built, and production began in 1921. Bentleys won the Le Mans 24-Hour races every year from 1927 to 1930. If it had not been for the war there might have been no Rolls-Royce aero-engines and no Bentley Motors Limited.

Blaze away

I bet you my pipe outlasts yours; it's filled with Bond of Union. It lasts about half as long again as ordinary mixtures.

They've got some sort of special curing process which slows down the pipe and develops the flavour at the same time.

It only costs 7d. an oz., but it beats any of the 8d. or 9d. mixtures I've tried.

Medium & Full **7**d. per oz.

Mild 7½d.

You can send Bond of Union duty free to your friends at the front. Order from your Tobacconist.

Before you pay 8d. for Tobacco try
Bond of Union
COPE BROS. & CO., LTD., LIVERPOOL AND LONDON.

Cigarettes and Tobacco

'PUT THAT bloody cigarette out!' Those were the last words of Lance Serjeant Hector Hugh Munro, better known as the writer 'Saki', before he was shot by a sniper at Beaumont Hamel one night in 1916. Munro did not give the order because he feared the risk of cancer, for in 1916 few understood what harm tobacco could do. He knew that the glowing cigarette was an aiming point for the enemy, as his own death proved.

Captain F.C. Hitchcock, of the Leinster Regiment, wrote that during a bombardment soldiers developed a craving for cigarettes. Few men could eat when under heavy shellfire – especially on the Somme, where exploding shells disinterred rotting corpses, and blew fragments of them into front-line trenches. The pipe-smoking lieutenant in the Bond of Union advertisement looks blissfully happy as the shells explode behind him. His stance and his expression say 'Trust me! I am a solid and reliable chap, and I am not panicking.' Advertisements for pipe tobacco often showed solid chaps like the lieutenant to suggest that if you smoked a pipe, you were a dependable, unflappable fellow. Some showed a public figure such as Lord Kitchener or Admiral Jellicoe, pipe in mouth. Tobacco was a

comfort, a relaxation and a sedative. When troops
were marching along the French country roads, a
thin film of blue smoke from pipes and cigarettes
would hang over the column 'like a pale spirit' until
it dispersed. The cartoonist Bert Thomas's poster
'Arf a mo, Kaiser!', drawn in November 1914, shows
a cheery 'old sweat' of the BEF lighting his pipe
before he shoulders arms and marches off to fight
Jerry. Pipes were classless. The poster raised over
£250,000 for the *Daily Dispatch* tobacco fund for
the troops. Padres would often take cigarettes to the
soldiers in the front line. Chaplain Geoffrey Studdert Kennedy, nicknamed 'Woodbine Willie' by the
men, described his ministry as taking 'a box of fags
in your haversack, and a great deal of love in your
heart'. Woodbines, one penny (0.4p) for a packet of
five, were cigarettes for the 'other ranks', and their
advertising was likely to be an enamelled-iron sign
outside the tobacconist's shop. Advertisements aimed
at officers, such as the ones for Kenilworth cigarettes, were more sophisticated. Both the Kenilworth
advertisements show a picture of a peaceful world,
where officers have wives or girlfriends, and a faith-
ful Aberdeen terrier. No Hun was going to come out
of the sun; there was going to be no dawn strafe.

The strain on pilots was just as great as that
on soldiers. In April 1917 alone, 207 Royal Flying
Corps pilots were killed. The man snuggling up
to the woman on the sofa is clearly a demobbed
officer, although not a guardsman, for it was 'not
done' for members of the Brigade of Guards to

Tatler, 12 June 1918, p. 303

..... *You've seen it through !*

You don't want to talk about it. You don't want to think about it. You just want to lean back and feel that the day you've been dreaming of since that first August of 1914 has come at long last.

It's good to be alive. It's good to be with her. It's good to sit at home, lazily watching the smoke curl up from your Kenilworth Cigarette,

and enjoying the flavour of that wonderful golden tobacco that suits the hour so well.

Peace finds Kenilworth Cigarettes unchanged, in size.

Kenilworth Cigarettes are made of mellow golden Virginia leaf yielding a fascinating aroma. They will compare favourably with any Virginian Cigarettes you can obtain, no matter how high the price. Yet Kenilworths only cost 1/4 for 20, 3/3 for 50, 6/6 for 100.

FOR THE FRONT.—We will post Kenilworth Cigarettes to Soldiers at the Front specially packed in airtight tins of 50 at 2/9 per 100, duty free. Postage 1/- for 200 to 300; 1/4 up to 900. **Minimum order 200.** Order through your Tobacconist or send remittance direct to us. Postal Address :—14, Lord Nelson Street, Liverpool.

Kenilworth Cigarettes

COPE BROS. & CO., LTD.,
LIVERPOOL AND LONDON.
Manufacturers of High-class Cigarettes.

Illustrated London News, 21 December 1918, p. 845

smoke Virginian cigarettes; only Turkish ones were acceptable. The copy suggests that the cigarette will help the officer to forget, but it will take more than a few Kenilworths to dull the memory of the early morning trench mortar fire and the cry of 'Stretcher bearers!' when the mortars have found their target.

Sources and Acknowledgements

The advertisements in this book have been reproduced from the following periodicals and collections:

Andrew Clark Collection (press cuttings), Oxford, Bodleian Library, 247927 d.68.
Bystander, Oxford, Bodleian Library, Per. 2705 d. 161.
Country Life, Oxford, Bodleian Library, Per. 384 b.6 36.1.
Graphic, Oxford, Bodleian Library, N. 2288 b. 7.
Illustrated London News, Oxford, Bodleian Library, N. 2288 b.6.
Land and Water, Oxford, Bodleian Library, N. 22281 b.3.
Punch, Oxford, Bodleian Library, N. 2706 d.10.
Punch, London, British Library, C.194.b.199 © British Library Board (pp. 9, 32, 50, 53, 74, 89, 102).
Sphere, Oxford, Bodleian Library, N. 2288 b.34.
Tatler, Oxford, Bodleian Library, N. 2289 c.1.

The authors would like to thank the staff at the following libraries for their invaluable assistance in the preparation of this book:

The British Library, St Pancras and, formerly, Colindale.
Peter Collins at Westminster Reference Library.
Mike Webb at the Bodleian Library, Oxford.

Further Reading

Bentley, W.O., *W.O., The Autobiography of W.O. Bentley*, Hutchinson, 1958.

Booth, Adjutant M., *With the B.E.F. in France*, Salvation Army, 1916.

Carrington, C., *Soldier from the Wars Returning*, Hutchinson, 1965.

Collins, D., *The Story of Kodak*, Harry N. Abrams, 1990.

Edmonds, J.E., *History of the Great War, Military Operations, France and Belgium*, 1914, Volume I, Macmillan, 1925.

Gilbert, M., *Winston S. Churchill*, Volume III: *The Challenge of War*, 1914–1916, Heinemann, 1971.

Gilbert, M., *Winston S. Churchill*, Companion Volume III, Part 2, May 1915–December 1916, Heinemann, 1972.

Graves, R., *Goodbye to All That*, Jonathan Cape, 1929.

Hitchcock, Captain F.C., *Stand to, a Diary of the Trenches 1915–18*, Hurst & Blackett, 1937.

Holmes, R., *Tommy, the British Soldier on the Western Front, 1914–1918*, HarperCollins, 2004.

Keegan, J., *The First World War*, Hutchinson, 1998.

Keynes, G., *The Gates of Memory*, Oxford University Press, 1981

MacDonagh, M., *In London During the Great War*, Eyre & Spottiswoode, 1935.

McLaren, B., *Women of the War*, Hodder & Stoughton, 1917.

Messenger, C., *Call to Arms: The British Army 1914–1918*, Weidenfeld & Nicolson, 2005.

Montagu of Beaulieu, Lord, and D. Burgess-Wise, *Daimler Century*, Patrick Stephens, 1995.

Mozley, J.K. (ed.), *G.A. Studdert Kennedy by His Friends*, Hodder & Stoughton, 1929.

Munro, H.H., *The Short Stories of Saki (H.H. Munro)*, Bodley Head, 1930.

Peel, Mrs C.S., *How We Lived Then, 1914–1918*, Bodley Head, 1929.

Sassoon, S., *Memoirs of an Infantry Officer,* Faber, 1930.

Sassoon, S., *Complete Memoirs of George Sherston*, Faber, 1937.

Warner, P., *Kitchener: The Man behind the Legend*, Hamish Hamilton, 1985.

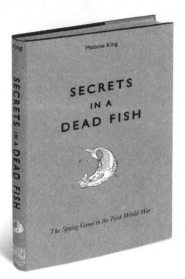

Secrets in a Dead Fish
The Spying Game in the First World War

Drawing on the words of many of the
spies themselves, this book is a fascinating
compendium of clever ruses that details the
extraordinary and sometimes hilarious lengths
to which spies went in the quest to communicate
secret messages in the First World War.

Available from all good bookshops, and
www.bodleianbookshop.co.uk

ISBN: 978 1 85124 260 3
Hardback, £8.99